SAYS YOU

a one act play by

j. andrew thomas

Also by J. Andrew Thomas

Suburban Purgatory Hell
Mauled by Death in the Hot Rain
Staring into the Void of Destruction
College is for Losers (Novel)
The Garden Gnomes are Watching
Sometimes You Get Lucky and the Problem Fixes Itself
Poems for Another Day
Cattle Prod (Novel)
All My Friends are on Television
Swallow God Swallow Nothing
With Pugs
The Bastards Will Always Win
Non-Union (Novel)
Ocean Currents (Play)
She Catches Her Breath in a Sob (Play)
The Greats are not so Great
A Place To Go When Things Went Wrong (Play)
Dead End Poems
Empire of Nothing (Novel)
Back to the Bars
Let Me Hold Your Heart Like a Flower (Play)
Dumb But Not Quite Damned
The Loud Thunderous Roar of Girls Searching For Invisible Love (Play)
It's Not Going to Get Better Only More Comfortable
Pitchfork (Novel)
Spring in Shamrock (Novel)
To Darkness Through a Wreath of Sudden Pain (Novel)
Wallowing in Obscurity

For a Second (Screenplay)
Nothing Doing Here There Anywhere
Bad Design
Her Candle so expire (Novel)
The Fat of the Day (Play)
Looking Down From Below
One Win Choice (Screenplay)
Spider in a Forest Fire
People Were Smaller Back Then (Play)
Super Busy Doing Absolutely Nothing
Three Porches (Play)
Sheep Drive
A Short Farewell (Play)
Hank and Emma and Sometimes Leo
We Should Not Expect Them to Be What We Want
Them to Be
The Protected Wild (Novel)
To the Crowd (Short Stories)
See the World Burn
The Tail End of (play)
Time Again Later
Some Peace (play)
from a flowerless land

Setting:

A dingy Atlantic City hotel room during a hurricane.

Characters:

Taylor
Paul

"I never could bear the idea of anyone's expecting something from me. It always made me want to do just the opposite."

— Jean-Paul Sartre

Says You

ACT I

TAYLOR:

Ugggh, look at this place! What are we even doing here? Why can't we just go home?

PAUL:

It's not that bad. It's practically free so who cares?

TAYLOR:

Cause it's a dump! No way I am staying here longer than a day. Uggggh!

PAUL:

Just relax! They say it's supposed to be over by tomorrow. And then they will open the casinos back up and well get that big suite they promised.

TAYLOR:

I knew when I heard hurricane last week we should have cancelled. I knew it!

PAUL:

I know, I know, I never thought they would close the casinos, first time I've ever seen that.

TAYLOR:

It's pretty bad out there. They told everyone to go home, which is what we should have done.

PAUL:

It's one day! We got booze and we got weed, so lets just bang and have a party! Then in the morning it will be gone and well have the rest of the weekend.

TAYLOR:
Maybe it's not too late, maybe we can make it out in time.

PAUL:
It's too dangerous. Just relax. Can you put down your bags already, it's going to be ok.

Taylor puts down her bags and lets out a sigh.

TAYLOR:
All I wanted to do was lay on the beach in the sun. That was it…just wanted to listen to my headphones and watch the ocean from my chair. That's all I wanted.

PAUL [*pulls out phone*] :
Look, see that forecast. Around three am it's going to clear and the sun will come rolling in. And guess what? Nobody will be here! Well have the beach to ourselves! And we've got one more day after that!

TAYLOR:
Let's hope so.

PAUL:
We had fun last night, right?

TAYLOR:
From what I can remember. What time did you go
to bed?

PAUL:
Around three I think.

TAYLOR:
Three! I don't understand why you have to stay up
all night and gamble, it's not like you ever win a
ton of money.

PAUL:
I know, I was on a roll for a while, I should have
stopped.

TAYLOR:
How much were you up?

PAUL:
At least 500.

TAYLOR:
And you ended up with?

PAUL:
Not that.

TAYLOR:
Did you win anything?

PAUL:
I didn't lose anything. After I won that big bet in
the beginning I was playing with house money all
night long.

TAYLOR:
I really don't see the point. You gamble that whole
time and you lose what you already had. Just take
your winnings and leave!

PAUL:
It's a game. Sometimes you get lucky and
sometimes you don't. Remember last summer,
Fourth of July, I won over a thousand bucks on
blackjack. And then I took you to that steak house
and ordered a 100 dollar bottle of champagne and
50 dollar steaks.

TAYLOR:
That was pretty cool. How much was that bottle of
champagne again?

PAUL:
It was like 150 dollars.

TAYLOR:
And those steaks, oh my god they melted in your
mouth. In hindsight we probably shouldn't have
blown most of it on drinks and food.

PAUL:
Eh, it's victory money, you are always supposed to blow it on stupid shit.

TAYLOR:
Yeah well we are still broke, so maybe if you win something this weekend we can put it in savings…you know, like adults.

PAUL:
That sounds incredibly boring. What the hell are we saving for anyway?

TAYLOR:
Oh, I don't know, maybe a house, a nice car, some furniture, you know, that kind of stuff.

PAUL:
I really don't see the point. You are going to graduate in a few months and we will be rolling in dough.

TAYLOR:
Yes, but not really. I'm going be in serious debt. You know this, I've told you a million times already. I'm over 300k now.

PAUL:
Yeah but whatever, well figure it out, it's not like we need to pay it all back right away. We can spread it out over 30 years like mortgage, right?

TAYLOR:

I have no idea. I keep signing new loan paperwork every year and it's so confusing. I think I have five different loans right now all with different interest rates. Everyone in class says we can bundle them all together when we are done at a lower rate so it doesn't matter right now.

PAUL:

See! There's nothing to worry about.

TAYLOR:

I wish I could feel that way. You know me, I'm always worrying. What if I can't pass the MCAT's? Then what?

PAUL:

Stop! [*grabs Taylor by the shoulders*] It's going to be fine! You will pass and you will be and awesome doctor making lots of money. Here, lets make a drink.

Paul opens a bag and pulls out champagne and orange juice.

PAUL:

Mimosas!

There is a loud crack of thunder.

TAYLOR:
Ah!

Taylor jumps and Paul isn't affected at all.

TAYLOR:
I'm amazed how nothing can bother you.

PAUL:
What, am I going to sit around and sulk on
vacation? Sure, the weather sucks but we can still
have fun.

*PAUL mixes two mimosas and hands one to Taylor and
she takes a sip.*

TAYLOR:
Thanks. What should we toast to?

PAUL:
To…our future plans…

They clink glasses, take a sip and kiss.

TAYLOR:
Plans? That makes it sound weird. Should have
been plan.

PAUL:
Of course, that's what I meant.

TAYLOR:
God I still can't believe this place. Ugggh, so gross.
I can't wait to have money so we will won't have to
live like this anymore.

PAUL:
What, you think I can't afford a better place? I can.
You know that.

TAYLOR:
So why are we here then?

PAUL:
I don't see the point in shelling out three hundred
bucks to sit in a room and get wasted.

TAYLOR:
See, that's what I don't get, this is the time to spend
money on a nicer room. We can't go out to the
beach and the bars, we are stuck here. So why not
get a nice, clean room?

PAUL:
It's one day!

TAYLOR:
I'm sure your parents would help you out if you
ask them.

PAUL:
Huh?

TAYLOR:
I know they still give you money.

PAUL:
It's not like I ask them for it. They know I don't
make enough at the restaurant to support us both.

TAYLOR:
Ok, but you never tell me how much they give you.
Why?

PAUL:
Why does it matter? It's my money. They give it to
me, not us.

TAYLOR:
We live together, we're engaged. Don't you think
we should have a joint bank account by now?

PAUL:
Here we go, again with this shit. Always prying
your way into my finances.

TAYLOR:
I have no idea how much money you have, spend,
make, I have no idea! How can I marry a man if he
isn't honest!

PAUL:
How the hell did we get on this? We're on
vacation!

Paul goes over and pours another mimosa.

TAYLOR:
It doesn't matter, you know it bothers me. I'm
completely transparent with my financial situation
with you. I'm not trying to shame you or anything.
I know your parents are millionaires and they
should help you out if you need it. All I'm saying is
I don't understand how you don't have enough
money for a nicer room. Are you gambling that
much of it away?

PAUL:
What? You don't even know how much they give
me! Maybe it's only a few hundred a month? Who
knows?

TAYLOR:
Oh my God, this is why I get frustrated, you do this
on purpose. You love having this secret and
holding it over my head. Whatever, I don't care. In
a year I'll be done school and I'll have a job and
you can do whatever the fuck you want. I don't
care!

Taylor starts to cry.

PAUL:
What the fuck! Already!

TAYLOR:
You will never understand.

PAUL:
Come on! You don't know what it's like growing
up like I did. My father always telling me to never
talk about money with people, always saying that it
changes the way people think about you…they will
always be asking for money if they know how
much we have!

TAYLOR:
Oh God that doesn't even make sense! You're
family has always treated me like shit because I
was poor. Sorry my father doesn't own this giant
college bar that rakes in millions.

PAUL:
Millions, haha, your crazy. They do make good
money yes but they aren't millionaires.

TAYLOR:
I looked up your parents house, it's worth 1.2
million. So that plus whatever money they have in
the bank plus the value of the bar, I'm sure they are
multi millionaires.

PAUL:
I'm pretty sure they don't own anything. They still pay a mortgages on all their shit, even the condo in Florida. It's a house of cards.

TAYLOR:
Ah, I forgot about that! Beachfront condo, that's easily 500 thousand! Right?

PAUL:
I don't know. I don't care. They say I'm not going to get anything when they die so I don't keep track. My dad will blow it all on some stupid bullshit, don't worry.

TAYLOR:
You really believe that?

PAUL:
My dad is adamant that I need to earn my own money. Our entire lives he told me and my brother Mike we wouldn't get any inheritance. So I believe him.

TAYLOR:
I doubt it. It sounds like something to motivate you to make something of yourself. I see so many stories about rich kids who are bored and don't work, they are all heroin addicts. They eventually overdose and die.

PAUL:
Yeah yeah, that was never going to happen with us.
My dad had me cooking in the restaurant at 10
years old. I worked my ass off while all my friends
were out playing sports.

TAYLOR:
Well that's taking it kind of far.

PAUL:
He's a maniac. That's why I can't go back and work
for him. Anytime I take a day off he gives me shit, I
can't take it.

TAYLOR:
I just wish you would go back to working full time,
we really need the money.

PAUL:
I'm fucking burned out. You don't know what it's
like working 60 hours a week in a hot kitchen. I just
need a little bit of a break. Another few months and
I'll be back at it. I promise.

TAYLOR:
Do you still want to open your own restaurant?
You never talk about that anymore.

PAUL:
Sure, that would be amazing. I just don't know
how to go about doing that. It's a lot of money and

work. It seemed more possible when I was younger. Now, I don't know…I've lost my zest for cooking. I need a breather. I would rather focus on your career, you know what I mean?

TAYLOR:
Yes but it can't all be about me. If you hate cooking, then try something else.

PAUL:
I don't know anything else! All my friends from high school, they have good jobs and nice houses and cool cars…what do I got? I'm not even a chef, I'm a god damn cook who can barely afford to pay the rent.

TAYLOR:
Who cares what other people have? I know you can cook your ass off, you are an amazing CHEF. Listen, once I get out of school, I say we move to a new town. We need a restart.

PAUL:
Where?

TAYLOR:
I think we should be closer to the city. All the good hospitals are there. The pay is better too. Maybe you could get a job at a fancy steak house or something.

PAUL:
I thought we were going to move back to West
Chamberlain when you graduated?

TAYLOR:
Did we ever decide on that? I know it was an
option but we never said one way or another.

PAUL:
Why not? I can go back to working at my dad's
place, finally make some real money again.

TAYLOR:
I'm kind of tired of living there. Don't you want
something different?

PAUL:
Look at where we are at now! It's different! And we
both hate living in Shakersville.

TAYLOR:
I had no choice, they pick where you do your
residency. It's not like we are staying there. It's a
cute little town if you think about it.

PAUL:
It's a bunch of hillbillies. I can't wait to get out. I
really hate working at that hole in the wall bar. I
didn't go to culinary school to fry up mozzarella
sticks and to make cheeseburgers. It's really

fucking with my head. I feel myself getting dumber by the day.

TAYLOR:
Three more months! What about living near Philly? I always liked Kimberford. It's like 15 minutes away and they have a good night life there. Lots of bars and restaurants.

PAUL:
That would be cool. It's going to be more expensive though. Since all those young people moved the rents have gone sky high there.

TAYLOR:
Well be fine. With both of us working I don't see how it would be a problem.

PAUL [*starts to get happy*]:
It might work. I've always wanted to live near the city. Ah man, imagine, we can be going to out to cool bars all weekend then we are only a short uber ride home! Or we can stay in town, there are a ton of places we can walk to and not have to worry about driving home…Fuck yeah. Man it's going to be so fun.

TAYLOR:
Yeah that will be fun for a while. We gotta save money though. Houses are expensive.

PAUL:
A house? With like a lawn and shit? Sounds like a lot of work.

TAYLOR:
It is, but it's worth it. Aren't you annoyed living around people? I just want to get away, I'm so tired of the whole community scene. I want to go to work and then come home to my own house and not have to deal with anyone. And a dog would be nice.

PAUL:
Jesus, you got this all planned out already!

TAYLOR:
You just were saying how jealous you are of your friends having nice houses. I thought that's what you wanted?

PAUL:
I do and I don't. I want a nice place to live but it's all the other bullshit. Fixing stuff, all the hassle of owning a house seems like a pain.

TAYLOR:
We can hire people if it pains you that much. I'm graduating in a few months, I'm ready for real life... finally. You try going to college for 10 years! I just want a paycheck. And to buy stuff. Nice stuff.

PAUL:
I guess.

TAYLOR [*frustrated*] :
God why can't you ever be excited about anything?

PAUL:
Because whenever I get my hopes up it never
happens. I am tired of getting excited. I just want to
live life and if something good happens…great! If
not, I won't be let down. It's so much easier that
way. Live in the present. Don't worry about the
future. Things will be what they will be. Be
happy…

TAYLOR [*interrupts*] :
I know, I know, be happy with what you got and
don't be sad with what you don't have. It's a stupid
saying. If we all thought like that we wouldn't try
for a better life. You have to try. Don't you get that?
It's not going to fall in your lap. I've been killing
myself with school for a long time and it's finally
going to pay off soon. And I did it because I didn't
want to be poor anymore. I had enough of that
growing up. I'm done.

PAUL:
Why are we doing this now? We're on vacation.
We should be having fun! [*drinks mimosa*]

TAYLOR:

I guess because you never want to talk about this
stuff. I have all these thoughts in my mind and I
can never voice them. And then as time goes by
they keep piling up and eventually I burst. I can't
hold them in forever. I know men can bottle things
up forever but women aren't like that. We are
emotional. I hate that I can't talk about kids with
you.

PAUL:
Jesus. What the fuck! How are we going to have
kids? We have no idea where we are going to live?

TAYLOR:
Who said anything about right now? I'm not
talking about right now. I'm saying in a few years
when we are stable. What's wrong with that?

PAUL:
Nothing…I guess.

TAYLOR:
I still think about what would have been if I didn't
do that thing back in college.

PAUL:
Thing?...[*remembers*] Oh, that. Yeah…well, it was
good we did.

TAYLOR:

Was it though? Maybe our lives would be totally different and we would be really happy now. You don't know.

PAUL:
Then how would you have kept going to med school? You couldn't have done it, it's too much work.

TAYLOR:
Well obviously I would have just gotten a job. Med school was never my dream. It just kind of happened. I would be totally fine working as a lab tech or something making 50k a year.

PAUL:
Then why did you spend all that money on school? You kept saying this is what you needed to do!

TAYLOR:
My professors talked me into it! I didn't know. They said I should keep going with school because a bachelors degree doesn't amount to much anymore. I didn't know what I was doing. And then when you get to a certain point, there's no going back. I mean, I'm happy I'm going to be a doctor making good money soon but it's not my dream.

PAUL:

I just wonder where we will be in life in a few
years. We could be living in another state or
something. Or another country, you don't know.
You really want to be tied down with kids like
that?

TAYLOR [*laughs*] :
Even if that's the case, and it's a big IF, it still
doesn't matter. I'm already feeling like I want them
so I know by the time I'm 35 I'm going to want to
get pregnant. It doesn't matter where I'll be in life. I
could be unemployed living in some little
apartment, it doesn't matter. You don't have to be
in this perfect spot in life to have kids. I know it
makes it easier but people make it work no matter
what.

PAUL:
I just seems like a lot of work. Look at how easy our
lives are! Won't you miss sleeping in every
weekend, going out to the bar, taking vacations
whenever…it's so easy! You add a kid to that, hooo
booooy, it's gonna be so hard to do anything!

TAYLOR:
Yeah I get how easy you have it. I really don't. I've
been busy the last few years with school so I don't
have the same feeling you do. Maybe once I'm
done and I get to rest a bit, I'll start to enjoy myself
and it will seem hard to give up our independence
but all I hear from my friends having kids is how

great it is. They seem so happy. I see their pictures
on Facebook and they seem so happy. And then I
start to feel bad, like, what the fuck did I do? I
could have a child right now, a little boy or girl,
seven years old and I gave it up because it was
convenient! I feel so selfish and guilty. Do you ever
feel that?

PAUL:
Not at all. It was the right thing to do at the time.

TAYLOR:
I used to think that but it's harder and harder to
justify it. If I could go back and change it, I would.

PAUL:
Really? You would give up on med school?

TAYLOR:
In a second. I think I think of it everyday now. I
can't get it out of my brain.

PAUL:
Jesus. That's crazy.

TAYLOR:
Sorry, what can I tell you? It was traumatizing.

PAUL:
Why now? You were fine for so many years.

TAYLOR:
I was never fine. No, *that's* crazy you thought that. I just pushed it away. Out of my life. And now I can't. Sorry.

PAUL:
So then what are you going to do?

TAYLOR:
I really don't know. Up my anti-depressants. Take more Xanax. Maybe try meditation when I get some free time which will be never.

PAUL:
Don't feel guilty. So many people have done it. It wasn't your fault, remember? It was mine, you said it was the worst time of the month for sex and I said it would be fine. Well, you were right.

TAYLOR:
Yes, but who knows though? I subliminally could have wanted to get pregnant! I was totally in love with you and was paranoid you would leave me, so a baby would keep us together.

PAUL:
Seriously?

TAYLOR:
Yes!

PAUL:
I can't believe you thought that.

TAYLOR:
We had only been going out for a short time. You were Mr. Rockstar. Maybe I did it on purpose. I don't know…I smoking so much pot back then. Who knows what I was thinking.

PAUL:
Rock star? It was a cover band…whatever. It's the past. We did what we did.

TAYLOR:
Well, you never answered my question…do you want a family someday?

PAUL:
I mean, someday…I think so…ummmm…sure.

TAYLOR:
That doesn't sound convincing.

PAUL:
I don't know, I'm like 60/40 right now, which is pretty good. I think I've warmed up to it much more than before.

TAYLOR:
That's it! So there's a 60% chance you want kids?

PAUL:
I used to be at 0% so that's pretty good!

TAYLOR:
Ok…I mean, what it's going to be like when we get older if we don't…I'm talking in our 40s and 50s. Just me and you? Doing what?

PAUL:
Anything we want! Well have a ton of money and we can travel all over the world doing cool shit. Everyone else will be tied down.

TAYLOR:
I do want to travel but that's not a reason to not have kids.

PAUL:
Look at the world. It's fucked. You really want to bring a kid into this fucked up world. We are barely going to make it out without seeing some sort of world ending nuclear war or a climate change disaster. We are fucked no matter what way you look at it. This next generation has no idea what they are in for. It's gonna be bad.

TAYLOR:
Maybe, maybe not. People always seem to find a solution to things. It's kind of our thing. We put it off as long as we can but when it comes to crunch time, we usually come together and survive.

PAUL:

I really don't see that happening. The whole world is fighting with each other about stupid shit. That's all we do. I'm so tired of it all. I just think about school…putting a kid through that hell…that's child abuse. I mean, it's got to be harder nowadays with all this social media. The kids can't even go home and get away from the bullies, they attack them online now. So many kids are killing themselves because of this shit.

TAYLOR:

So that's it? We give up? We stop reproducing as a species because it's hard? I HATED school as much as you did. I know I had it much worse than you did. We had no fucking money. I had to wear the same clothes day, day out, had no money for lunch, it sucked! But whatever, I got through it and it made me tougher. I look back and am glad it wasn't easy. I see the popular kids I went to school with now and most of them are losers! They had it too good. They thought life was going to be a breeze because it was so easy in high school and they get to college and they ended up dropping out after the first year. It was awesome seeing that!

PAUL:

Let's just give it some time. See where we are at in a few years.

TAYLOR:
See, that's the problem, I can't wait that long. If I give you another few years and then later you say you don't want kids, then I have lost all that time! I will have to start over finding a husband and then I might be 40 by then!

PAUL:
You think ahead too much. Maybe I'll come to an epiphany some day. I'll wake up and realize my life is incomplete. Right now I don't feel that way. Do you?

TAYLOR:
Not right now, but I know it's coming. I know it. I can feel it with all my being. I don't want to be an old spinster. I have seen those women and that's not what I want. Not that there's anything wrong with that. I just know it's not me.

PAUL:
Well, that's you, I don't live life like that. I wake up and take life as it comes. Maybe that's why you have so much anxiety. You are worried about everything.

TAYLOR:
Yeah well most successful people wake up and set a plan for themselves for the day. They don't float on by and hope everything works out. Sorry. I may be anxious sometimes but I try and use it as a

motivator. If I work my ass off today and get all of
my things done, then I can relax at the end of the
day knowing I did my best.

PAUL:
So what, I'm a lazy slob? That's what I'm hearing.

TAYLOR:
Oh god. I didn't say that.

PAUL:
You try working eight or 10 hours in a hot kitchen,
seven days a week. Try it. I bet you don't last a
week. You know how much I worked in my 20's. I
was killing myself!

TAYLOR:
You think the world has treated you pretty badly,
don't you?

PAUL:
Huh?

TAYLOR:
Always the victim, it's never your fault.

PAUL:
It's not. I never wanted to cook. I got pushed into it
by my father. I am the oldest, so he wanted me to
follow in his footsteps. I sometimes wish I was born
second. My brother Max was so lucky, he didn't

have any pressure on him. Being the baby, Mom and dad doted on him constantly, they coddled him and let him do whatever he wanted. I should have just gone to college like a normal kid. I hate my father for that.

TAYLOR:
You told me you never wanted to go to college, you said you hated school! And I quote "Why would I go to college when I can have the same experience and not have to take any classes," is what you would say all the time.

PAUL:
It made sense at the time. I was young, I was having fun being in a band, working at a college bar. I didn't realize how much of a job cooking would become once we moved out of West Chamberlain. I fucking hate it now. I really do.

TAYLOR:
It's called growing up! We can't keep partying our whole lives. You say you want to be like your brother Max, well, Max is always working. He's got tons of money because he never stops working!

PAUL:
Yeah I know. You know what it's like having a little brother who is a millionaire? Who is good at everything, who is best friends with my father? No, you don't. Everything Max touches turns to gold.

Everything. I hate him. I really do. It's just not fair.
We have the same fucking DNA and look at our
lives! He's not even 30 for Christ's sake!

TAYLOR:
You think he's happy? Trust me, he's not. He's
addicted to work and money. It's never enough. He
barely sees his kids. Just talk to his wife, she will
tell you.

PAUL:
That's not remotely true. He takes them all over the
world with him. They were in France two weeks
ago. I showed you the pictures! It looked amazing!

TAYLOR:
And I bet he's working the whole time. Last
Christmas he said he works 80 hours a week on
average. Uggh! You can have that. What's the point
in having all that money if you can't enjoy it? Oh
and remember that last time I saw her over the
summer she said they hadn't had sex in a year!
That's a dead marriage if you ask anyone.

PAUL:
I didn't believe that then and I don't believe that
now. She's such a liar.

TAYLOR:
I do. He's probably having sex with hookers. He's
got that apartment in the city where he stays

during the week. You know he's doing something there. So ridiculous.

PAUL:
I really don't care, it's not my business. It's his life. All I know is Max said he wants to retire at 40, so I guess he's going to be relaxing then. For now, he's going to work his ass off so he doesn't have to later.

TAYLOR:
Well see. Those kinds of people, they can't retire. Money is a game to them. Actually, it's not even money to them, it's numbers. They wake up with a number and the game is to try and make that number as high as possible for that day. That's it. They don't know what they will do with it, all that matter is MORE and MORE and MORE. It's an addiction. It's a sad addiction.

PAUL [*sulking*] :
I just feel like such a loser most of the time. I barely talk to my father anymore. He gave up on me. I don't know what you see in me anymore. I have nothing going on. I can't even keep a job. All my friends growing up have great jobs and big houses and everything going for them. But at least I have you. God…without you I would probably be homeless.

TAYLOR:

You're not a loser! You are so smart and talented,
you just need a change.

PAUL:
I'm just afraid of making another mistake. I can't
afford it. Time is running out.

TAYLOR:
The only way you succeed is to fail. You talk to any
successful rich guy, they all have failed a million
times.

PAUL:
You sound like motivational books my father
reads. I've heard it all before. You either got it or
you don't and I don't have it.

TAYLOR:
You should have more confidence in yourself.
What about opening up your own restaurant?

PAUL:
How the hell would I do that?

TAYLOR:
Get a business loan? People do it all the time. Then
you can do whatever you want.

PAUL:

I don't know, that's a lot of pressure. What if it fails? You do know 90% of new restaurants fail. It's so fucking hard to pull off.

PAUL:
You have your dad. He could give you advice. Maybe even back you with money. Have you ever asked him?

PAUL:
Fuck that! I can't ask him for help. I can't grovel like that. I need to get something on my own or it won't be real. And if he had any money in it, I would have to listen to him about everything. I can't do that if it would be my place. Nope, no way.

Taylor sighs.

TAYLOR:
So it's ok to take their money when there's no strings attached.

PAUL:
Boom! You figured it out! I didn't ask for it. They just send it. So that's on them. If I ask for say 100 thousand to start my own business, then that becomes a problem. A few hundred bucks a month is nothing to them. They know you aren't making anything. So what's the harm? What's the fucking harm Taylor?

TAYLOR:
Fine! Whatever! Don't work. Three months and we are out of here and hopefully you will figure something out! I know I'll be fine. I've had to do everything on my own my whole life anyway so I'll be fine!

PAUL:
See…you always do this shit. You always pull that parent card. Like you are better than me because you're parents are gone. You know I was thinking about it and I'm actually jealous of you.

TAYLOR:
What?

PAUL:
Yeah, I'm jealous. You don't have anybody to report to. You don't have anybody lording over you, keeping watch, making sure you are making the right decisions. You don't have a safety net like me. You are your own person. When you make a decision, it's yours. You don't have to think about what your parents will think. It must be very freeing. It's no wonder you are so successful. God if I didn't have a nice big ol' net below me, in case I screw up and fall, I would be light years beyond where I'm at now in my life.

TAYLOR:

What the hell? You have no idea what it's like not
having parents. It's awful. I feel very alone a lot of
the time. All I have is you. I wish I had family to
take comfort in. To see on the holidays, to go and
visit, to call up and tell them how things are going
and to tell them I love them. I DON'T HAVE ANY
OF THAT AND IT SUCKS! You have all that and
you have no idea how god damn lucky you are. No
idea. And this whole "light years ahead" what the
hell is that? So does that mean you are only with
me because you can't do any better? That's what I
take that as.

PAUL:
No, why would you think that? I meant with my
career. We would obviously be together. You are
the best thing in my life, I would never give that
up. All I'm saying is I wish I stayed in college. I
wish I majored in something with computers or
graphic design and if I did I would probably have
some kick ass job right now instead of being where
I'm at. A dead fucking end.

TAYLOR:
With me.

PAUL:
I'm in a dead end. You're not. And you're right, I
shouldn't have said that about your parents. I'm
stupid. It's just something I think about from time
to time. They put so much pressure on me. I know

I'm a failure in their eyes and it kills me. I sometimes think I drink so much because I feel like such a loser. It's hard having a father who is a millionaire. It's big shoes to fill.

TAYLOR:
And a brother. I get that. I do. I don't have anything to live up to. It does make things simple. But I would rather have screwed up parents around than none at all. That's for sure.

PAUL:
You can share mine! Things will work out. I feel better talking about this. It's been weighing on me for a while now.

TAYLOR:
Alright, have it your way. Just know I love you Paul...I believe in you.

PAUL:
Thanks, that means a lot. Come here.

Paul pulls Taylor in. They kiss for a minute and the lights go out. A minute later they turn back on and Taylor and Paul are under the sheets after having sex.

TAYLOR [*remote in her hand, changing channels*] :
I can't believe the summer is already over. It's so depressing. We always have so much planned and

when it's over we look back and nothing much
happened. Don't you hate that?

PAUL:
It goes way too fast. Spring it rains the whole time
and it's cold as shit until mid May and then we get
a week of 70's and then it's 95 degrees until
September and we get another 2 weeks of nice
weather and then cold and rainy again. It's such
bullshit. We should pack up and move down south
next year. What do you think?

TAYLOR:
I haven't really thought about it. Where would we
go?

PAUL:
Florida. No taxes, weirdos everywhere, beaches,
bars, it's seems like such a party. Don't you think?

TAYLOR:
It gets really hot in the summer. The bugs are the
worst. I think one of the Carolina's would be better.
It gets down to the 50's in the winter which isn't
too bad.

PAUL:
Hey, as long it gets me out of here, I'm good.

TAYLOR:
Won't you miss your family?

PAUL:

What? They don't care about me. No, my mother
does. She would be sad. But my dad won't care and
Max lives part time in New York so whatever. It
would be nice to leave everything behind, start
over.

TAYLOR:

Am I going with you?

PAUL:

Of course! [*kisses her on the head*]

TAYLOR:

I didn't know this is what you meant by "not sure
where we will live." I thought you meant
somewhere in Pennsylvania, like 20 miles from
your parents.

PAUL:

I used to want that but not anymore. I can live
anywhere now. I don't care.

TAYLOR:

Well, I have to think about this. I don't know if I
want to move. I have all my friends here.

PAUL:

They are just friends, you will make new ones. It's
not like you have any family. So what's the
difference?

TAYLOR:
When you don't have family, friends are all you
have!

PAUL:
Friends are bullshit, they always leave you. When
something comes along in life that benefits them
more than you, they will leave in a second. They
won't even think about it. My family is your
family.

TAYLOR:
Well, I'm glad we're going to be married. I know
you didn't want to at first but it makes me happy. I
can't lose you.

PAUL:
I'm not going anywhere [*lights cigarette*].

TAYLOR:
You can't smoke in here!

PAUL [*exhaling smoke*] :
Nobody is here, take a chill pill.

TAYLOR:
Yeah that's true. Can I have a drag?

PAUL:
You sure? What about the nicotine tests?

TAYLOR:
They aren't random. I'll be good until December
and then after that I can't chance it.

*Taylor takes the cigarette and takes two puffs. Paul takes
it back.*

PAUL:
Just take a whole one, I have plenty!

Paul reaches for another cigarette and lights it.

TAYLOR:
I shouldn't.

PAUL:
Just take it, what's the harm? It's only one.

TAYLOR [*taking a drag*] :
God that's good. I miss this so much. But smoking
everyday like I used to, I can't do it. I did just read
Gwyneth Paltrow smokes one cigarette a week. She
makes it like this special treat. I would do that.

PAUL:

I would hate that. All week I would be looking
forward to 5 minutes of enjoyment. And then when
it was over I would be very depressed.

TAYLOR:
I was really hoping you would quit with me. How
about after I graduate. We both stop cold turkey
and never smoke again.

PAUL:
Maybe, well see.

TAYLOR:
It's hard for me to see you smoking, I really want
one every time! If we did it together I think we
could really do it this time. When I'm at work I
never even think about it and then I get home and I
smell it on you and see you go outside and I'm
tempted again.

PAUL:
I know I could quit if I wanted to. I did it for a few
months before. I just don't know if I'm ready.
That's a big commitment. Like, never again? Fuck.

TAYLOR:
Why not at least try?

PAUL:
You don't get it. It's different for me. I'm a cook.
We all smoke. It's just part of the industry. Look at

my dad, he's 66 and quit a year ago! You know
why? Because he finally stopped working in the
kitchen! You should see breaktime, it's just a cloud
of smoke on the back porch of the restaurant. It's so
fun. Just give me some more time. Maybe when I
move into a manger role at some point.

TAYLOR:
How long will that be?

PAUL:
Who knows? Maybe soon! I don't know what my
next move will be. I could do it.

TAYLOR:
But don't you feel like your going to die every time
you smoke? I feel that way. Like, here's the
cigarette that's going to put me over the edge, I'm
finally going to get cancer now.

PAUL:
No, not at all. People smoke for 50 years and they
are fine. Besides, it's not lung cancer that will get
you, no, that's only 15% of smokers get that. It's the
emphysema that fucks you up. You get that and
you're done.

TAYLOR:
I don't want any of it. I don't want to die young or
be talking through a hole in my throat with one of
those voice box machines when I'm 63. You ever

seen that commercial with that lady who looks like a corpse?

PAUL:
Yeah, it's frightening. I always change the channel, I can't look at that shit.

TAYLOR:
Remember being 18 years old, not having a worry in the world…we could eat anything, drink anything, smoke as much as we wanted. There was no thought of anything bad happening. Except getting fat. God, I took it for granted. That's what I hate the most about getting older, constantly having to worry about our health. We were invincible and now we aren't. And I know I'm not even 30 yet and people tell me all the time I'm not that old to be complaining but I feel old. And that's really all that matters. It's what you *feel*.

PAUL:
I still feel like I'm 19. It's like I'm the same age but I've been taken out of my element. If I was transported back in time 15 years with my exact body and mind, I would have no problem living exactly the same.

TAYLOR:
Really? You don't think you've grown at all? You don't even go out anymore.

PAUL:
Because everyone is gone! Who am I going to hang out with? The town we live in feels like death. I can't wait to leave.

TAYLOR:
What about me?

PAUL:
That's different. That's relationship shit. I mean when I was raging every weekend. Drinking beer, playing shows, hooking up with girls, it was a different world. I could go back to that in a second if I wanted to.

TAYLOR:
So what's stopping you? If this is what you think about all the time, why are you in a relationship. I don't think about that stuff.

PAUL:
Like I said, I'm 35, it's over. Everyone has kids and shit. I've accepted that this is my life.

TAYLOR:
Wow. Wow. You make me feel so good. Like I keep you locked away. You are free to go. Don't let me keep you down.

PAUL:

Would you stop, you brought this shit up. All I'm
saying is that I still feel young, what's wrong with
that?

TAYLOR:
It just sounds like you wish you were happier…like
before you met me. That's all.

PAUL:
It's not like I'm saying it was better, it was just
different. I'm happy with you now and I was
happy back then. Does that make sense.

TAYLOR:
Happier before or after we met?

PAUL:
After.

TAYLOR [*laughs*] :
Good answer!

PAUL:
If we didn't meet I would probably be on drugs
and homeless by now. Like I said, I need you. You
keep me stable and grounded.

TAYLOR:
Awwww. See, that makes me feel better.

TAYLOR:
I'm going to get a shower, not much else to do.
Want to join me?

PAUL:
Nah I'm good. Feeling lazy right now.

TAYLOR:
Ok, you're loss.

Taylor gets up and goes to the bathroom and closes the door. The shower starts to run.

Paul rummages through his suitcase and pulls out a small bag of cocaine. He dips his pinky in and snorts some. He does it twice more and quickly puts it away. Then he sits on the bed and turns on the TV to the local news.

PAUL [*to audience*]:
Fuck!

Paul rubs his nose and shakes his head like a dog shaking off water.

PAUL:
Shhhh! Don't tell anyone. I'm not addicted or anything. I just do it here and there. Like a cup of coffee. Heightens my senses. Makes me feel a little

bit alive. Like gambling. I really don't know why it's such a taboo thing. Cocaine has been around for a long time and unless you get a bad batch or do it with non-stop intensity of a raving lunatic, you're not going to die. I really wish they would legalize all drugs already and lab test them so we know they are safe to do. That would make everything so much better. But they don't want to do that. They make too much money busting people. And it would cost too much money and take too damn long to set up an workable infrastructure around it. The government can't do shit. It is kind of sexy and dangerous though. You buy a bag off some friend of a friend and you hope it's ok. You hope there isn't fentanyl in it. And you take that first snort knowing it could be your last. It's like Russian Roulette. Literally.

Paul snorts another line.

I usually don't do it this fast but I'm in a time crunch. Taylor will never get it. She's never worked in the restaurant industry. Everyone does it. It's a shit job and we have to go, go, go all night long. It's a necessary evil. Truckers are the same way. They are all hopped up on Adderall and coke and whatever else will keep them driving 18 hours a day. You want your shit, you let us smoke and do drugs. Then you will get it without complaint. It will magically show up and us losers will die young and we won't ever get any credit for keeping this society well fed and comfortable.

Whatever. It's all non-sense. This whole life. I'm so ready for it to end. I have no direction. I have no joy. I have no anything except disdain for 99.9% of people. And I used to love people! That's what's so crazy. I was a people addict. I couldn't get enough. I used to have so much fun, ALL THE FUCKING TIME. And now, ugggh, nothing. I'm 35 and I feel like I'm 60. Life is routine and boring and there's never any money to do anything. I wish I never left West Chamberlain. I don't know why we couldn't just live apart for a while. Why did we have to play house? Oh, I know why, Taylor said she would be lonely out there all by herself. In that hick town full of idiot rednecks. I told her I didn't want to go but she forced me.

It's only been nine months and I'm crawling out of my skin. I can't make it another three! How the hell can I tell her I have to get out? She will freak out. I feel bad though. She needs me. She can't be alone. If I leave she will lose her shit. And I don't even want to break up! All I want is some time to myself, to figure shit out. It's an impossible situation.

I feel bad that I lied to her. I have talked to my father. I told them about the shit job I was working at the local dive bar down the street, frying up wings and making cheesesteaks and he begged me to come back and work for him. He said I'm wasting my talents. He said his manager just left and I could run the restaurant if I wanted. Said he misses me and I needed to come home. "You can live here rent free for a while, just come back, you and Taylor!"

It was weird. He never talked like that to me. He was so friendly and inviting. I miss him. I miss West Chamberlain. I miss the young girls walking down the sidewalk. I miss the energy of living in a college town. Taylor knows I've always wanted to go back. She could get a job at a nearby hospital. She doesn't want to though. She never got along with my family. I guess they thought I could do better or something. They acted like they liked her but she could see through it. She's not dumb. I feel bad. I know she's the one but if we don't have some time apart I don't think well make it. I just need some time. It's been too long. Going on eight years now!

Something did happen too…when I went back to visit my parents for a weekend. Taylor was too busy with her residency shit so she stayed back. I met up with some high school buddies and we all went out drinking. God, I can't even say it. I'm too ashamed. It was good though. Gave me a jolt. You know what I'm saying. You know what happened. And even though I feel bad, I don't regret it. It was fun. It was like the old days. I didn't even know her name! Now that's living life. Not this sitting around waiting for things to happen. Waiting for a job and money and making plans where to live. That's…business…right? That's not living everyday to the fullest. That's the mundane shit they tell you will kill you in the end. Whatever that means. I don't know. I'm fucked up.

Oh and there's no way we can have a kid. No way. I can't do it. I'm too young. I have too much I want to do. Why the fuck does she want a kid anyway? Life is so much easier without them. It's non-stop bullshit! You never get a break! Who wants to live like that? I'm too used to this lifestyle now. A baby would mess everything up.

Paul lights a cigarette and takes a drink.

It feels good to be alone. I hope she's in there for another half hour. I don't know what to say to her anymore. It always turns to an argument. It's how we communicate now. It's our natural way to speaking to each other. I fucking hate it. I don't even know why I put up a fight anymore. I always give in at the end. I let her have her way. Always. She never gets that. She always wins.

Maybe not today though. Today I'm feeling different. I'm tired of lying. I'm tired of pretending everything is ok. It's not. I'm not happy. I'm not fucking happy anymore and that's all that matters.

I used to think that I had to put Taylor's happiness above mine. That to be a real man you needed to keep a woman happy and then you would be happy. Now I know that's not true. It's my happiness that matters most. You have to love yourself before you love someone else and I don't love myself anymore. I don't even know who the fuck I am anymore! I wake up and feel like I'm trapped in some weird dream and I can't wake up. I'm fucking trapped!

The shower turns off.

PAUL:
Shit.

Paul puts some coke on his pinky and snorts it and puts the vial back in his bag.

PAUL:
I don't know. Maybe I'll wait until the weekend is over. Why turn this into a nightmare? What's another two days? The casino will probably be open tomorrow so we can at least have one good day down here. And then we will go back home and I'll think of a way to tell her what I need to say.

Taylor comes out of the bathroom brushing her teeth.

TAYLOR:
What are you watching?

PAUL:
Stupid news. I don't know why they put these weathermen out in hurricanes, it's so stupid!

TAYLOR:
One station does it and the rest think they have to do it to keep up. It's like when it snows, they just want ratings.

PAUL:
They were showing all the looting going on in the city when you were in the bathroom.

TAYLOR:
Really.

PAUL:
Yeah, people busting windows stealing whatever they could carry. Some people had carts full of TV's and electronics. It was funny seeing them running through the rain and everything was getting soaked. Shit was probably ruined.

TAYLOR:
It's crazy how we act civilized 99% of the time but one little thing happens and we turn into wild animals fighting for survival.

PAUL:

If I was poor and I looked out my window and people were doing that I would probably partake.

TAYLOR:
I'm so tired of people. This is the kind of shit that makes me not want to live anywhere near the city. Too many nutjobs out there.

PAUL:
I know but what are we supposed to do? Live out in the country? There's nothing to do out there! It would be so boring. Maybe I'll get a gun.

TAYLOR:
A gun? And do what? Walk around with it in the front of your pants? You will probably end up shooting yourself instead!

PAUL:
Stop! You act like I'm an idiot! I've shot guns my whole childhood, my dad brought us up with them.

TAYLOR:
I've never seen you shoot one.

PAUL:
It was fun for a while but it was never my thing. Besides, I know you hate them.

TAYLOR:

So why bring it up? I think you like to rile me up
on purpose.

PAUL:
The world is nuts! I want some protection. If we are
going to live near the city I want to feel safe.

TAYLOR:
Get some mace or something. I don't want a gun in
my house. You get drunk too much, something will
go wrong, I know it.

PAUL:
Is this about your dad?

TAYLOR: I didn't have a gun in the house he
would still be alive. I think about him everyday.

PAUL:
Maybe.. But don't you don't think he would have
just killed himself another way?

TAYLOR:
No, no, I don't think so. He was drunk and angry
and depressed. I've read so much about people
who shoot themselves in the head, they all want it
to go away quickly. If he didn't have access, he
would still be alive. He wasn't going to hang
himself. He would have woken up sober and
would have been happy to be alive. I hate guns.

PAUL:

Ok, ok, I get it. I won't ever get a gun. I promise.

Taylor hugs Paul and lays on the bed next to him.

TAYLOR:

Thank you, that means a lot. You don't know what it's like [*kisses Paul*].

PAUL [*getting up*] :

No, your right. God damn I'm hungry. You want a grilled cheese?

TAYLOR:

That's our only option, huh.

PAUL:

And some chips here.

Paul throws the chips to her and pulls out a little George Foreman grill and plugs it in.

TAYLOR:

I can't believe you still have that thing. Nobody uses them anymore!

PAUL:

I don't care what anybody says, this is the greatest cooking invention of all time. If I was stuck on a desert island and all I had was this thing and a pocket knife, I would be totally fine.

TAYLOR:
Where would you plug it in?

PAUL:
Ok, if I was stuck in a hotel room in Atlantic City in
the middle of a fucking hurricane, I would be
totally fine. Better?

Paul begins to put together the sandwich.

TAYLOR:
You do make a mean grilled cheese on that thing.
Better than most restaurants.

PAUL:
I put in my 10,000 hours with this thing, living in
that apartment with Brent and Justin back in
college. God what a way to live! We were such
drunken slobs, it's amazing how we survived.

TAYLOR:
Yeah well I remember your mom was always
dropping off home cooked meals. You had it
pretty good living so close to home but getting to
party like a college kid.

PAUL:
I know, I'm aware how lucky I was.

TAYLOR:

Still are.

PAUL [*agitated*] :
Yes. I'm aware. I'm not a baby. I can do things on
my own. I'm not a dummy.

TAYLOR:
What? Who said you were?

PAUL:
I hear it in your voice, you think I'm spoiled.
You've said shit like that before.

TAYLOR:
I don't think you're spoiled, I think you're lucky.

PAUL:
A dumb lucky bastard. Right?

TAYLOR:
What is going on? Why are you starting a fight.

PAUL:
Sorry, I am a little sensitive about being made fun
of because of something I can't control. Sorry.

TAYLOR:
Who said you are dumb? I never said that.

PAUL:

You are always telling me I should go back to school and get a degree. Like I'm stupid or something.

TAYLOR:
You are always complaining about your job! So I said go to school and get a degree or learn a trade or something. I can't believe we are doing this again!

PAUL:
You say that knowing I won't though. You love being the smart one. Am I going to have to call you Dr. when you graduate?

TAYLOR:
Why would you do that?

PAUL:
Sometimes I think you are only with me because it makes you feel smart.

TAYLOR:
What? What the hell is going on with you?

PAUL:
You heard me. You like being with an idiot. It makes you feel smart. I get it.

TAYLOR:
Well, that's not true because you're not an idiot.

PAUL:
Compared to you? Of course I am. I have a high
school education. I cook food for a living…barely. I
can barely read at this point.

TAYLOR:
That's so crazy! You are crazy if you think that! I
can't play guitar…I can't do all that computer stuff
you do with music, I can't fix cars and house stuff
like you. Didn't you get like 1300 on your SAT's?

PAUL:
Around that, but who cares?

TAYLOR:
That's better than I did!

PAUL:
Well, in the eyes of the working world, I don't have
a college education. So I'm useless. What the fuck is
playing a guitar going to do for me in the real
world? All those hours I spent and now it's
meaningless. Fucking joke. I should have been
studying. I got straight C's in high school by doing
nothing, if I had studied just a little bit I would
have had all A's. My parents didn't care so I didn't.
It's more my mother's fault. Fucking booze hound.
She was more worried about dinner parties and
fancy clothes and expensive purses. What the hell

was that? Why have kids if you are going to ignore them?

TAYLOR:
My mother was working three jobs to keep us afloat, so don't tell me about feeling abandoned. I was home alone most of the time after age 12. It was normal.

PAUL:
Yeah I know, I know. Everything I say you have an answer for. You really are something else.

TAYLOR:
Do you even love me anymore? You are so mean sometimes.

PAUL:
Christ, here we go. Listen, I left my family so we could be together. I did that for you. If I didn't love you I wouldn't have moved to another state so we wouldn't break up. I had it so good back in West Chamberlain. If it wasn't for you I would still be living there, working at my fathers restaurant, probably managing the whole place by now, so don't say I don't love you, that's bullshit. I changed my whole life for you.

TAYLOR:
Wow that sounds like more of a punishment! And guess what, I gave up the whole college experience

for you! You were my first and only boyfriend. I
missed out on so much stuff.

PAUL:
Who asked you to? You came onto
me…remember? You were all about dating an
older guy who was the lead singer in a bad…whose
dad owned the coolest bar in town and could get
you and your friends in even though you were
underage…remember?

TAYLOR:
Yeah well that was stupid of me. I was a dumb kid,
I'll admit that. You were cool. You were
mysterious. Girls flung themselves at you like you
were Jim Morrison or something. You could have
had any girl you wanted but the wrap was you
didn't date girls, no you only hooked up with them
for a bit and then it was onto the next one. And
then it was my turn. It was late at night and the
pizza shop across the street from the bar was
packed. I was paying for my pizza when I realized
I didn't have enough money. Please can I have just
one slice I said drunkenly to the counter man. You
must have heard me because you came up behind
me and paid for my pizza. "You are my hero!" I
said giving you a big hug. Then you asked if we
wanted to sit with you and your band and that was
that. We went home together and the next morning
you asked me to be your girlfriend. I felt like I won
some lottery because you decided to date me. And

then when everything settled down a few months later, when all the excitement was over, I realized there's no mystery to you. You are just a nerdy guy who was pretending to be cool like everyone else. You're just as fucked up as the rest of us. And I loved you more because of that! I wanted that real guy inside the whole time. I wanted you! That's the guy I fell in love with, not the rock star guy who could have any girl he wanted. The real Paul. The guy who told me he felt like a loser in high school because he played Dungeons and Dragons and programed computer games. That guy.

PAUL:
Yeah well I've been running away from that guy my whole life. He's dead.

TAYLOR:
I've seen him, he's very much alive. You are a total dork and you know it.

PAUL:
I guess it doesn't matter anymore. I'm on my way to 40 and nothing much matters. I'm a loser and have always been a loser. I don't know why you want to marry me anyway.

TAYLOR:
You always do this! Don't put down yourself!

PAUL:

Aren't you tired of this? All this fighting? It's all we do anymore. We're on vacation and instead of having a good time we're fighting. I'm so tired.

TAYLOR:
Of course! I don't want to fight anymore than you do. What should we do? You tell me, I never know how we get into these things.

PAUL:
It's like we don't look at life the same way anymore. Things have definitely changed.

TAYLOR:
Oh yes. But change is good, right? We still want the same things, right?

PAUL:
Do we? We can't even decide where we will live. I have no idea what I'm going to do for work. You will be graduating in three months and can get a job anywhere. It's kind of scary.

TAYLOR:
It's going to be fine! Don't worry.

PAUL:
I do. I do worry all the time. I worry we won't stop fighting and then well get married and buy a house and have kids and then well get divorced and it will be horrible!

TAYLOR:
Jesus, you are thinking about that?

PAUL:
Yes. I'm very scared.

TAYLOR:
Ok, so then what? What do you want to do? What's
the solution? Therapy? Couples counseling.

PAUL:
I don't want to do that. Not right now. Maybe we
should take a break…I don't know. I don't know
what else to do.

TAYLOR:
Break…I don't think so. No, if we do that we won't
ever get back together.

PAUL:
Why? People do it all the time.

TAYLOR:
I know you. You will go off into Paul world and
forget about me. I know it. We can't. Let's just
relax. I'll calm down. I'll be less bitchy. I promise.

PAUL:
There's just so much pressure. All the time. Don't
you feel it?

TAYLOR:
No! I don't get that feeling at all.

PAUL:
I guess I feel trapped. I want to figure my life out
and with us, you know, where we are, I can't.

TAYLOR:
It's a few more months. Please, just let me graduate
and then we can do whatever you want. I can work
wherever. It doesn't matter.

PAUL:
I don't know if I can last that long. I'm so depressed
all the time.

TAYLOR:
I'm trying here!

PAUL:
I'm sorry, I really am. I can only be me. I'm fucked
up. Maybe we can take a break, see how we feel.
Absence makes the heart grow fonder, right?

TAYLOR:
I don't believe that, no. You will go off and do your
own thing and that will be that. I don't understand
what you want to do. What can't you figure out
with me around?

PAUL:
I want to see what it's like to be alone. I want to see
if it will make me happy. We've been together so
fucking long I don't remember what it's like.
Maybe I'll be happy…I don't know. Maybe I'll be
completely miserable and then I'll know we were
meant to be together. The only way I know that is if
we separate for a while. And I mean total
separation, we don't see or speak to each other.

TAYLOR:
So what then…I can't even call you? What if it's
something important?

PAUL:
Like what?

TAYLOR:
What if I get sick or something. Or get into a car
crash and am in the hospital. Wouldn't you want to
see me?

PAUL:
Oh God, that's not going to happen. I need a
month. How's that. One month, let me figure
things out.

TAYLOR:
That's a long time!

PAUL:

I thought I was being generous. I could use three if we're being honest.

TAYLOR:
Three months! That's a break up, that's not a break. You really don't like me anymore, do you?

PAUL:
I'm going through some shit right now, don't you see that? I'm out of my head with this.

TAYLOR:
It's always something with you. Why do I have to always be the rock? I'm tired of being the strong one. You think I'm not exhausted by everything going on right now? I just want to be done with school and start making money and live in a nice place and enjoy life. That's it. We are so fucking close. Why can't you see how good it will be?

PAUL:
That's all great for you but I still won't be happy. I need a change. I don't know what that is yet but I need to get out of this rat race for a while and figure shit out. Why can't you see that!

TAYLOR [*shakes her head, puts hands on her face as she sits down away from him*] :
I don't know why I care so much. You're right. You won't be happy...ever. So yeah, fine, go off, do

what you want. I can't fight anymore. It's too
much. I hope you have a good life.

PAUL:
What the fuck? It's a month! Just relax!

TAYLOR:
I've seen this before, I know what it is. You do a
small break and then after a month goes by it will
be easier to dump me. I know what this is, I'm not
dumb. Nobody ever gets back together. It's fine, it's
fine, I don't care anymore. I'll be fine.

PAUL:
Come here.

*Paul tries to pull her in for a hug but Taylor pushes him
away.*

TAYLOR:
No, don't touch me. We aren't doing this. You
don't want me anymore. I just can't believe we are
stuck here. FUUUUUUUCK!

Taylor goes to the door and looks outside.

TAYLOR:
You couldn't have waited until tomorrow? God, I
need to get out of my mind.

Taylor pours vodka into a plastic cup and chugs it coughs. She pours another glass and chugs it.

PAUL:
What the fuck are you doing? You are going to be sick!

Paul grabs the bottle away from her.

TAYLOR:
I just want to pass out and wake up tomorrow, ok?

PAUL:
You are going to puke! And then you will be hungover tomorrow.

TAYLOR [*starts to cry*] :
Who cares? Who cares!

Taylor falls onto the bed and puts a pillow over her head. Paul tries to console her but she pushes him away and screams under the pillow.

The lights go dark and 20 seconds later they come back on.

It's about an hour later. Taylor is by the door smoking a cigarette, watching the storm with a drink by her. She has a blank look on her face. Paul is laying on the bed, watching TV with a drink, also smoking.

PAUL:
So you ok?

TAYLOR:
I'm fine. I should have seen this coming.

PAUL:
I really don't know what else to do.

TAYLOR:
Let's not get back into it. We keep talking in circles.
I'll be fine. The vodka is doing it's job. I actually
feel kind of happy.

PAUL:
Really?

TAYLOR:
A little. Like, now I can do whatever I want. It's
kind of nice.

PAUL:
Exactly!

TAYLOR:
I want to start painting again. It's been so long, I
miss it.

PAUL:
You should. I should have never stopped playing. I
think that was my downfall.

TAYLOR:
Guitar?

PAUL:
Yeah. I don't know why I stopped. It was so stupid.
I loved jamming.

TAYLOR:
So start playing again! What's stopping you?

PAUL:
Seems pointless. I got no band. I need a band or it's
like I'm strumming into the wind. Nobody fucking
cares.

TAYLOR:
I'm sure you can find some people who would play
with you.

PAUL:
Maybe.

TAYLOR:
Or a band that needs an amazing singer or lead
guitar player. Your band was pretty big for a
moment, I'm sure people still remember.

PAUL:

Big for a bar cover band I guess. I wish we would
have recorded that album of original music. I had
some good songs. Sucks.

TAYLOR:
It's not too late!

PAUL:
Yeah it is. The moment is gone. The energy is gone.
Youth is gone. You need to strike when the iron is
hot. I should have put everything into that band.
Fuck. Anything I do now would be forced. It would
be lame. I'm so done.

TAYLOR:
You are ridiculous. You are only 35. You act like
you're an old man!

PAUL:
I am compared to 22. I can barely function. Nothing
seems important. Remember when everything in
life was so important? Remember that? Every
decision seemed like it was life or death and
now…now…now we know none of it fucking
matters.

TAYLOR:
Yes, that's true. But things were important back
then. Whatever path you chose at 18 years old
would affect the rest of your life…potentially. I
remember talking to my guidance counselor before

I graduated high school and he was asking what I wanted to major in. "I have no idea!" I said. He shook his head and told me I needed to really think about it because if I picked the wrong one I would end up working at a grocery store! Can you imagine saying that to an 18 year old! Who the hell knows what they want to do their entire lives at 18! I just didn't want to get picked on at school. That's all I cared about going into college. A fresh start. New classmates. Living on my own. That was it. Parents put all that stupid pressure on us.

PAUL:
It still seemed like life mattered more though. I just think of all that time we had in front of us. It seemed endless. 30 seemed so far away. Nothing could hurt us. And now, it's all downhill. Fuck.

TAYLOR:
I really wish you would go back on antidepressants. You were so much better.

PAUL:
Fuck that. It's not real. I would rather be depressed than fake happy. I don't know how you take those things.

TAYLOR:
Because they work! It keeps me balanced.

PAUL:

Yeah but your problem is anxiety. It's different.
Depression is so much worse. You have no idea
what it's like wanting to die all the time. It's awful.

TAYLOR:
Oh ok, yeah anxiety is so easy to deal with!
Hahahahahaha! You have no idea what it's like. It's
like that feeling of being on the edge of a
cliff…ALL THE TIME! It's always doubting
yourself, wishing you would fail so you wouldn't
have to do it anymore, thinking, if I fail this
test…my life will be over, I'll be nothing! Nobody
will ever love me. Why does he stay with me? You
don't matter. You aren't pretty. What's that thing
on your face? A pimple? Ahhhhh! Everyone will
look at it and they will secretly be laughing at you.

PAUL:
Ok, I get it, I get it!

TAYLOR:
You don't. It's all day like that. You might be
depressed but you are calm. You might be
apathetic about life but it's better than having a
hyperactive brain that you can't handle.

PAUL:
So you were like this for years while we were
together. You seemed fine.

TAYLOR:

I put on a good face. What can I say, I'm a good
actor! We eventually become our true selves, we
can't help it. It's only a matter of time.

PAUL:
Right.

There's a long pause. Taylor lets out a sigh.

TAYLOR:
I don't know why we can't just start over, you
know?

PAUL:
No, I don't know what you mean.

TAYLOR:
We start over. [*gets excited a little bit*] We break up,
ok, and then we find our own apartments and then
we go out on a "first" date and pretend we never
met. We do the whole thing over!

PAUL:
What?

TAYLOR:
It's perfect! We clear the slate, we put all that crap
that we fight about in the garbage. You can have
your independence and I can have mine. We go
back to having fun!

PAUL:

It sounds good on paper but I don't know. It seems kind of crazy.

TAYLOR:

Exactly! We need to do something big! Something nobody else has done before! We still love each other, we know that, it's just we are tired of each other. Your right, we need a break. We will do our own thing during the week and can hang out on the weekends. Like old times.

PAUL:

Yeah but I thought you wanted a commitment. I thought you were worried about wasting time. What if we do it for a year and it still doesn't work out? Won't you be pissed?

TAYLOR:

I can't see it not working out. Like how? Remember that first year together? It was amazing!

PAUL:

Let's take it one step at a time. [*pause, thinking*] I mean…like what if we don't live near each other. Then what?

TAYLOR:

I'll go wherever you go, I don't care. I can work anywhere. Doctors are in need all over.

PAUL:
Well I'm probably going to go back and live with
my parents for a while.

TAYLOR:
What? Why?

PAUL:
My dad said I could go back and work at the
restaurant. I can save some money and get paid a
good salary.

TAYLOR:
Oh my God. Really? I knew it…I fucking knew it!

PAUL:
What does it matter to you? I'm not allowed to live
where I want to live now?

TAYLOR:
You will never grow up. Good lord, I don't know
what I was thinking.

PAUL:
Sorry I'm not going to be a doctor. Some of us have
to take what we can get in this world.

TAYLOR:
It's not even about that. I already know what's
going to happen. I'm so stupid. God I'm so stupid.

PAUL:
What's going to happen? Please, fill me in.

TAYLOR:
You're going to start dating college girls again!

PAUL:
What!?

TAYLOR:
Don't act so surprised, I know you. You miss the whole college scene. I get it.

PAUL:
I'm 35 years old. What college girl would want to date me?

TAYLOR:
You look and act like you're 25 so I would think plenty. Now it all makes sense...wow, it all makes sense...

PAUL:
You get these things in your head, you sound so crazy.

TAYLOR:
No wonder you were talking about playing guitar again. You're going to start another band, aren't you?

PAUL:
You said I should!

TAYLOR:
Not while your living at home and playing in front
of young girls! I meant outside of West
Chamberlain! Like Philly or something.

PAUL:
You know how hard it is to find adults who want
to start a band? It's almost impossible. I bet I could
put up a flyer or a craigslist ad and have 20 kids
banging on my door to start something. And they
got time and energy like you wouldn't believe.
Anybody over the age of 28 is done. It's all about
work and money. It's death out there. Plain and
simple. People hate their lives. You can't create
good shit with people like that. You need to have
your heart into it 1000%.

TAYLOR:
You sound like an idiot. You are never going to be
a rock star, I'm sorry to tell you. It's not going to
happen.

PAUL:
Maybe, maybe not, who's to know. I just want
some time alone. Time to give it another go. A year.
Tops.

TAYLOR:

And then if it doesn't work out we get married.
[*scoffs*] It's like I'm the consolation prize. The loser
path of life.

PAUL:
Or everything works out and I take over my dad's
business and start a great band and we get married.
Why can't that happen?

TAYLOR:
Because it won't. I don't fit into that life. You will
find somebody new. I know it. What the hell did
your dad say to you? He wants you to take over the
restaurant now? What the fuck?

PAUL:
I called him a few days ago and told him I quit my
job. He freaked out and said I needed to come back
and work with him.

TAYLOR:
When were you going to tell me this?

PAUL:
Now I guess.

TAYLOR:
What the hell else don't know! All these lies! You
were planning this whole time!

PAUL:

I wasn't planning anything. I was surprised he offered. You know much he wanted me to fail after I left. I assumed he would have laughed and me and hung up the phone.

TAYLOR:
You knew. You knew he would break down and sympathize with you. He's your dad for Christ's sake. Father's love their sons.

PAUL:
Not as much as Mike. He's the favorite.

TAYLOR:
You say that but I don't think so. You were first born. That's why he wanted you to follow in his footsteps. Did he ever encourage Mike to be a chef?

PAUL:
Mike always hated it…and Mike's too smart for that kind of work anyway. My dad knew that.

TAYLOR:
I'm pretty sure you are smarter than Mike.

PAUL:
No way.

TAYLOR:
Oh for sure. Mike's a talker. He's not that smart. He seems smart but he's not. I would know.

PAUL:
Oh, I forgot you know everything.

TAYLOR:
I don't but this I'm an expert at. I've been going to
one of the best schools on the east coast for years
now. You know how many smart people I come in
contact with on a daily basis?

PAUL:
I'm guessing a lot.

TAYLOR:
No! You would think that but nope, nope, nope. I
would say half the people there are actually really
intelligent people. The rest are a bunch of fakes. So
many cheaters, god it's disgusting. If you can talk
you can get through most of it. Especially the men.
It's like a bro frat thing these guys have with the
professors, I can't stand it.

PAUL:
That's kind of scary.

TAYLOR:
It is. But whatever, it is what it is. What I've learned
is that a lot of doctors kind of wing it. It's all trial
and error. Science seems like it would be black and
white but it's not. They call it the "art of science"
for a reason. It's very subjective. You can have a

headache and go to 10 different doctors and they will give you 10 different answers and most likely they will attribute it to whatever field they are in.

PAUL:
I get that. That's why I don't go to doctors. It's all a scam. Everything is fine until you go see some quack and they find shit wrong. Like getting your car inspected. They have to find problems to make money. Fuck em. I hope you won't do that shit.

TAYLOR:
Hey, we are paid to look. Don't make us the bad guy. It's funny, I read that most doctors won't get treatment if they are dying of cancer. They would rather just die quick than draw it out. So funny.

PAUL:
Weird.

TAYLOR:
Not really. When you see people suffering everyday and how bad life is like that, you don't want to go through it. Besides, once these guys can't do their job anymore, they don't want to live. They love being in power. They won't ever give in and be the patient, they hate it. It's all about power with them, it's crazy.

PAUL:
And yet, you are going to be one of them.

TAYLOR:

Yes but I won't *be* one of them. I'm not going to get wrapped up in that ego game. You know me, I'm as humble as can be!

PAUL:

You were. Things are changing though. I see the stars in your eyes. You want the good life. You see it. It's close. You want that fancy penthouse apartment in the city one day with the door man and a life of maids and assistants and nannies. You want that don't you?

TAYLOR [*laughs*] :

You make me out like I'm this vapid person! I live within my means! I don't know what's wrong with having a nice life if you work for it. And I've worked my ass off and haven't asked for a dime from anybody. Have I?

PAUL:

I guess not.

TAYLOR:

And where do you get off accusing me of wanting to be some rich socialite city doctor? You grew up in a mansion with endless wealth!

PAUL:

I didn't ask for that! I wanted to get away from that. That's why I moved away with you. Duh.

TAYLOR:
Well, not anymore. Guess you weren't cut out living the normal life. Apartment living sucks, doesn't it. Time to go back and suck off daddy's teat.

PAUL:
Fuck you. I'm so sick of your shit.

TAYLOR:
Excuse me?

PAUL:
I tried being nice but apparently you don't want to be friends. So fuck it. I don't give a fuck what you do. Let's just end it. This is never going to work.

TAYLOR:
Finally, we get to the honest truth. Like I said, you wanted to let me down gently. We go on a break and live separate lives and then I just fade away. You wouldn't even have to break up with me. I would probably break up with you! That's what you wanted you fucking coward! I at least deserve an honest dumping. Go for it, I'm strong now. I can handle it.

PAUL:

You just make shit up in your head all the time. You should really be a writer. You have so many crazy stories, you would sell so many books! How the hell do you know what I'm thinking?

TAYLOR:
I just do, ok. I know you. You, like most men, are simple. You eat, you sleep, you jack off and you drink. That's it. You see a pretty girl and you want to fuck her, you see a pizza on TV you want to eat it, you see a trailer for a comic book movie, you want to see it. It's not that complicated.

PAUL:
You know me alright. Good lord, what the hell is wrong with you? If I said some blanket statement about women like "damn chicks all they want to do is go shoppin! they sure love their shoes!" I would be a sexist. Right?

TAYLOR:
Yes…I see your point but…

PAUL:
Just stop. Stop trying to win. Just leave it be.

TAYLOR:
So that's it then. You are moving out when we get home. I don't even know if I can afford the apartment on my own. Do you even care? Have you thought about me at all?

PAUL:
Yes, but what am I supposed to do? We're not married. I go my way and you go yours.

TAYLOR:
Eight years together and you don't care about me at all!

PAUL:
I need to take care of myself first, I'm sorry. It's about my happiness first. Not yours. I know that sounds harsh but that's how life works.

TAYLOR:
I'm not stupid. I know how break ups work. I just don't know how people can one day shut a person off like that. I could see if it was a few months. But eight years! I don't deserve a "let me know if you need anything." If it was me leaving, I would definitely let you call me for a few months if you needed anything. Sorry I don't have a job and am living on school grant money right now. I can barely get by.

PAUL:
I'll ask my dad, I'm sure he can help.

TAYLOR:
Of course…[*snickers*] Of course. Always running back to daddy when you need out of a jam. He can

keep his money. I wanted you to step up but
apparently you can't. It's fine. I'll figure it out.

PAUL:
You know what, fuck you! I tried. Fuck you! I'm
getting the fuck out of here. God I wish we never
came here!

Paul goes to the door and opens it.

PAUL:
Look it's letting up! Maybe we can leave!

Taylor goes to the door and peeks out.

TAYLOR:
There's no way we are able to drive home. Look at
the street, it's covered in sand!

PAUL:
Fuck that. I can drive over that.

TAYLOR:
How? You will get stuck.

PAUL:
It's not like snow.

TAYLOR:
You've been drinking!

PAUL:
Who cares, nobody is out. What's going to happen.

TAYLOR:
I'm not going anywhere. You can go.

PAUL:
How will you get home?

Taylor goes back and sits on the bed.

TAYLOR:
I'll uber or something. Don't worry about me.

PAUL:
You're really going to stay here?

TAYLOR:
Yes. I'm not going to die in a crash.

PAUL:
It's going to be fine!

TAYLOR:
Go ahead, see what happens.

Paul throws his clothes in a bag and heads for the door.

PAUL:
Last chance!

TAYLOR:
I'll see you in a bit. You aren't going anywhere.

PAUL:
Fine, whatever.

Paul leaves.

TAYLOR:
Idiot.

The stage goes dark and a light is on the bed. Taylor lies down.

TAYLOR:
God why did I come here? I'm so stupid! I could be at home right now, all nice and cozy on the couch, watching TV with a cup of coffee. Maybe I'm dead and this is hell. Or I'm in some twisted episode of the Twilight Zone. I'm only two hours away from home and I feel like I'm on another planet…FUCK!

I know I should just end it. Walk away. He's right, this relationship has run it's course. We need a break. It's just so hard. We talked about the future for so long and how much better it would be once I graduated and I'm so damn close now! Why can't we just make it a few more months and see how it will be? That's all I'm asking. We can get out of this Podunk redneck town and move somewhere cool.

Get a nice apartment, go out on the town, meet some new people.

I should have seen this coming. Paul has been going downhill for a while now. I was too involved with school to notice or care. I figured he would pick himself up and get out of his rut on his own. I wonder how long he was planning on breaking up with me? How long has he been miserable? It's not like we stopped having sex like all my friends have. We still do it at least twice, sometimes three times a week. I know so many couples who literally don't have sex anymore. I don't get it. And they don't seem to care. I told my one friend Stacy her husband is definitely cheating on her because he's a traveling pharma salesman and they haven't had sex in a year. "Even if he is, whatever, as long as I don't hear about it, what's the difference?" My mouth dropped to the floor. She really didn't care. She has a nice life and no money problems and lives in a big house so she is happy. It's crazy. Crazy, crazy, crazy.

I don't think Paul is or has ever cheated. I would know. I catch him looking at young girls when we are out but that's it. I bet he misses dating all those young girls. He loved feeling like a rockstar. I don't blame him, it's got to be intoxicating. But if he thinks he's going back to that life when he moves back to Kleggsburg, he's gonna see real quick that things are different now. You can't go home. Sorry

Paul. It's a fact. The past is gone forever. No matter how much we want it back, time has passed us by. You are going to be 36 next year! You can't date 22 year olds!

He will try though. Maybe he will trick a few into bed. But once he tries to date them, he will see, there will be no connection. They are different people. This new generation coming up, they are the cell phone generation. They can't function like the rest of us. I got lucky, I just missed it. I can still read books and walk around without looking at my phone every two seconds, which makes me very happy. He will see. Try talking to them for more than a few minutes. They have no attention span. They will pull that phone right up to their nose and nod and pretend they are listening. It's really something else. They are like drug addicts.

Maybe that's what he needs. He needs to see how bad it is out there. Maybe that break will give him a wake up call. After a few months he will come running back when he remembers how good he had it with me. Maybe. I don't know. I don't know fucking anything anymore. I had it all planned out perfectly and now? I'm going to be living alone in some town I hate for three more months. Ugggh. He's not taking the cat either. I know he loves that cat but he's not taking Edvard anywhere. Yes I know it's a weird name for a cat but I named him after my favorite painter. And it suits him because he's a cat who can be sweet as can be and one minute later can be totally crazy. Like Munch. But that's probably a lot of cats since they are really wild animals that we tamed just enough to keep them from killing us in our sleep. It's true. If house cats were as big as lions, they would eat us if they got pissed off enough.

It's funny I never thought about life without Paul before. It's always been him. All I had in my head was us going through our whole lives together until we are in our 80's, and that image of us, gray haired, sitting on our porch, holding hands in our rocking chairs, waiting for our grandkids to come and visit. It seemed so romantic! And now…now what? It's all gone. Poof! Just like that. Once this storm passes, we will leave here and go back home. Paul will pack his stuff. His dad will probably send movers and a truck. He won't have to lift a finger. We will hug and he will say he will call me when he gets home but he won't. He'll text something and then that will be that. Maybe I'll call him a few days later and he won't answer and then I'll find something he left behind and ask him if he wants me to drop it off and he'll say "leave it out on the porch, I'll pick it up tomorrow," and he'll stop by when I'm at work. And that will be that.

I wonder if he will go to my graduation? He said he wanted to be friends. A friend would go. [*pause*] Of course he won't go. Why would he? He will be

fucking some young girl by then. God I'm so stupid
for even thinking that!

I just need to focus on myself and school. I don't
even want to think about dating anyone. I need
some time to figure things out. I always wanted to
go to a therapist. That might be the way to go. See a
shrink for a while, get all my shit out and then
when I feel better, I'll present my new self to the
world. If I just run out and try to find a guy now, it
won't go well. I'll come off as desperate and guys
hate desperate. They only want what they can't get
and I don't have the self esteem for that game right
now.

Taylor gets up and opens the door and looks out.

Ugggh. It looks like it's getting worse now! Haha, I
knew it! Look, he's coming back! *[points outside]*

*A minute later, Taylor steps back and Paul comes
running in, drenched with water and sand.*

TAYLOR:
I told you!

PAUL:
Fuck it's bad out there!

TAYLOR:
What happened?

PAUL:
I got the car started and I start driving down the street through all the sand and I'm thinking I'm going to make it out…and then some fucking cop in an SUV pulls me over! He tells me all the roads are closed until tomorrow and to go back to the hotel!

TAYLOR [*laughs*] :
Of course you idiot! You are lucky he didn't get you for drunk driving!

PAUL:
I think if that happened I would have been the first person busted for DUI in a hurricane. [*pauses*] FUCK! I could have made it to the highway if it wasn't for that pig!

TAYLOR:
It's supposed to be done tomorrow so well leave then.

PAUL:
Hopefully.

Paul gets a cigarette and lights it and stands by the door. Taylor does the same.

PAUL:
Back at it, huh?

TAYLOR:
I mean, why not? My life is over and I'm so fucking
stressed right now, I need something.

PAUL:
You look good, you know. I miss seeing you
smoke. That was always a big attraction for me.

TAYLOR:
Why? It's a pretty gross habit.

PAUL:
You seem cooler. I guess because it seemed like you
didn't give a shit back then. You were loose.

TAYLOR:
Loose? I was never a whore!

PAUL:
Not like that! I meant you were more carefree.
Everything wasn't so planned out. You weren't
anxious all the time about everything.

TAYLOR:
Yes well med school will do that to a person.

PAUL:
Sucks.

TAYLOR:

So if I start smoking again you will think I'm hot?

PAUL:
I never said I wasn't attracted to you!

TAYLOR:
But you thought I was easier to be around. Like I'm
wound up tight now. Right?

PAUL:
Like you said, it's got nothing to do with smoking.
You got stressed out from school, I get it.

TAYLOR [*looks at cigarette*] :
This is making me feel better. It's the smell though,
I can't deal with smelling like shit all day! Maybe I
can vape. You ever try it? Then I won't be nagging
you to quit.

PAUL:
Don't do anything. You were doing so good
quitting. Don't start back up.

TAYLOR:
I guess it doesn't matter at this point. We're done.
It's going to be weird not having you around. I
mean, we've seen each other everyday for over
eight years now.

PAUL:

For sure. It will be hard at first. Big change. [*lights another cigarette, stares out the door*]

TAYLOR:
You seem unaffected by all this. Like catatonic.

PAUL:
No, I have a million emotions running through me right now. I just keep everything bottled up. I can assure you I'm feeling quite suicidal.

TAYLOR:
Then tell me! Let it out!

PAUL:
Why? I'll sound like a crazy person. I'm 95% sure I'm making a mistake breaking up with you. I know I'm going to end up living in a homeless shelter someday, hooked on drugs and you will be living in some big mansion on the main line with a husband who's a lawyer or something and three kids living the dream. And I'll regret ever taking you for granted.

TAYLOR:
So you're saying there's a 5% chance that this is the right decision? Why do it then? Let's stick it out for another few months…right?

PAUL:

I told you, I can't. I'm literally going to die if I stay
in that apartment any longer. I need to leave. And
again, it's not you, it's me. I know that sounds
cliché and it's a cop out but it's the truth. I'm going
out of my fucking mind…

TAYLOR:
Ok, ok, I get it. You know me, I'm a problem solver
by nature. I see a problem and I look for ways to fix
it.

PAUL:
But relationships don't work like that. You can't
just fix them like that. They are like living beings.
They need to be coddled and given love. It's like
their food. We starved ours to death by not giving a
fuck anymore. We did that.

TAYLOR:
So now it's my fault? I thought you said it was your
fault? I'm so confused.

PAUL:
Yeah, we killed the relationship and now I want to
leave instead of trying to bring it back from the
dead. That's what I meant. I don't want to try
counseling and go through all that. I can't. I don't
have it in me. That's on me. I'm sorry.

TAYLOR:

Oh that's such crap! I tried for so much longer than you to keep the passion going! I always wanted to go out on the weekends and travel and do fun things. You kept saying no, no, no, all you wanted to do was go to the movies and have mechanical unloving sex and watch TV. So after years of trying to get you to do anything, I gave up. I said "fuck it," lets stay on the couch. I'll go out with my friends and focus on school and Paul can stay at home and be comfortable and when I'm not doing any of that stuff we can hang out at home where he's happiest. That's the truth.

PAUL:
I fucked up, ok! I don't know. I'm depressed or something. That's why I'm leaving. You shouldn't have to deal with my shit anymore. You should be happy now!

TAYLOR:
Always the victim. [*mocking*] My depression, my depression, waaaaah! You can't help yourself. Be a fucking man! Get help if it's so bad. How many times did I tell you to see a doctor? Hundreds of times!

PAUL:
I'm going to now!

TAYLOR:

Yes, yes, now that we are broken up, you will fix your brain and be a great boyfriend to some lucky gal. Meanwhile I've lost eight years. Eight years I'll never get back! I could be married by now. You know how hard it is to meet somebody good now? All the good guys are locked up. They are engaged or married. I'll have to look for guys in their late 30's who are divorced.

PAUL:
That makes no sense. You are only 29. You can get a younger guy in his early 20's.

TAYLOR:
Not really. It's different for women. I'm considered a cougar now to those kids. Men date younger, women date older. And older is 35 to 40 with baggage. Kids.

PAUL:
Women want to mature in life. They want to grow, they are always wanting to level up. Marriage, job, house, kids, all that. You can't just sit and be happy with life in the present.

TAYLOR:
Like you? You sit around and are miserable. Probably because you are so bored. You need goals in life. You strive for them and then when you reach them you feel happy for a bit and then you set new goals. What's wrong with that? Men do

that too! Successful ones! I can't wait until you move back home. I give it a week and you will be calling me to get back together. It's going to be a real wake up call for you. Things have changed. Everyone is gone. All those people you worked with and those girls who worshipped you, ALL GONE!

PAUL:
You don't know anything.

TAYLOR:
I do, that's the problem. I know too much!

PAUL:
Did you know I fucked some 21 year old girl when I went home a month ago? Huh? Did you know that?

Taylor pauses, waiting for him to say it's a joke but Paul just looks at her, waiting for a response.

TAYLOR:
What? That's not true.

PAUL:
Yes it is. It was great.

TAYLOR:
Fuck you. Even if it is true, which I don't believe, that's gross. You're fucking gross.

PAUL:
Why? We're both adults. I told her I was 23 and just graduated and she believed it!

TAYLOR:
Holy shit. You did. I can't believe you. I'm so stupid. [*puts hands in her face and sits down and begins to cry*] No wonder you want to leave. God I can't believe this! I'm so stupid!

PAUL [*feeling bad*]:
No, I'm stupid. I'm an idiot. I'm the asshole.

Paul tries to comfort Taylor but she pushes him away.

TAYLOR:
Don't fucking touch me! Don't ever touch me again!

PAUL:
I'm sorry.

TAYLOR:
No your not. You are such a bad person. How the hell could you do that?

PAUL:
I was drunk. I didn't even know her name. You know?

TAYLOR:
No, I don't know Paul. I'm not like you. I don't go
out and get fucked up and bring strangers home
and fuck them and then go back to my fiancé and
act like nothing happened. No, I don't know what
you mean you fucking shithead.

PAUL:
I deserve that.

TAYLOR:
21? Good lord. I just…you know what this means?

PAUL:
Ummm…maybe…

TAYLOR:
I can't ever trust you again!

PAUL:
I get that.

TAYLOR:
You wanted this. You wanted to sabotage this
relationship. You probably wanted to tell me right
away and didn't have the guts. You knew you
could use this to push me away for good. I mean,
not at the time, at the time you were drunk and
wanted to fuck a college girl. But then you figured
if you ever needed to break up our engagement,
this would be like dropping an atom bomb. There's

no coming back from this. But you knew that already. You knew that was the one thing I can't handle.

PAUL [*sarcastically*] :
Yup, you figured me out. This was my whole sinister plan. What the hell do you take me for? Some evil genius?

TAYLOR:
Maybe, I thought I knew you but now, I have no idea. I'm staring at a possible sociopath who could have been cheating on me for years. Do you have some kids out there I don't know about?

PAUL:
This was the only time, I swear!

TAYLOR [*sighs*] :
What does it matter? One time or a thousand times!

PAUL:
That's a big difference. Having sex with a thousand women behind your back? That would be some feat.

TAYLOR:
See…you don't even care. Eight years together and it's all a joke to you.

PAUL:

It's not. I'm just as fucked up about this as you are.
I don't show emotion like you, sorry. I clam up and
hold it in and then when you aren't around I'm
going to be driving around thinking about veering
into oncoming traffic because I am a worthless,
horrible human being who can't accept love.

TAYLOR:
That's a good one. You can't take love in, like my
love I give you is oil and you are water, it's
bounces right off. But I bet if some new hot girl
says she loves you after a month of dating, I bet
you will accept her love. Won't you? Just say it, I
you are bored and you want to move on. It's fine.
I'm going to be fine.

PAUL:
Yes you will be fine. I bet you will be married in
less than a year to some good looking rich doctor.

TAYLOR:
That would never happen. I hate them. Bunch of
narcissists playing God. I'm good. I'm going to be
by myself for a long time. I can't jump into
anything. I can't even imagine a world where you
aren't in it. I'm still trying to figure what that's
going to be like. I guess you already are there.
What was it like? Kissing someone new? Did you
feel guilty or was it exciting?

PAUL:

You sure you want to talk about this? This is weird.

TAYLOR:
Yeah, why not? Maybe it will help me hate you more. Then I can move on. I don't think we can be friends. I need to hate you.

PAUL:
Ummm…yeah it was definitely strange. Exciting at first and then guilt sets in a little later. Like I couldn't fully enjoy it. Which made me feel better. Like I'm not some unfeeling monster. I wish I never did it. You gotta believe me.

TAYLOR:
Oh I believe you. It's easier to ask for forgiveness than permission, that old line. But I think you are still secretly happy you got to bang some college floozy. You can think about that girl whenever you want now. Maybe even do it again when you go back home!

PAUL:
No, I think I'm going to take some time to myself. Like you. I need a breather.

TAYLOR:
You should. It will clear your head.

PAUL:
So you're going to be ok?

TAYLOR:

I don't know. I'm feeling better but I'm far from ok.
You are still here now so I have no idea. All I can
picture is you leaving and I'll be there alone. Alone
again. In that old house.

PAUL:

You can do whatever you want with it now.
Decorate it, arrange furniture, get that cat you
always wanted!

TAYLOR:

Yea maybe. Still going to be weird. A cat might
help. I would get an orange tabby like I had as a
kid and name him Cosmo.

PAUL:

See, that's something you've wanted to do, now
you will get to do it!

TAYLOR:

But then what if we get back together? Will I have
to get rid of the cat?

PAUL:

It's fine, I'll deal with it, just do what you want to
do.

TAYLOR:

And I hate those sounds at night. I'm pretty sure
the place is haunted.

PAUL:
Maybe they are friendly ghosts?

TAYLOR:
I wish I could get a big dog. Something that would
scare the shit out of anybody who comes to the
door. You realize it's going to be hard to sleep. I'm
going to feel like every noise is someone trying to
break in.

PAUL:
It's three months. Winter will barely be starting by
the time you are out of there.

TAYLOR:
And then moving again. Uggggh. I think I'm going
to throw everything out except my clothes. I need
to start over. I can't keep schlepping the same shit
I've had since forever. I need all new stuff.

PAUL:
Sounds like a good plan.

TAYLOR:
Who knows. We make plans and they go to shit
anyway. So what's the point?

PAUL:

It's all we can do. Hope for the best, expect the
worst. You know?

TAYLOR:
Just promise me if I call you, you will answer or at
least call me back. Because if I do, then I really need
to talk to you. Don't cut me off totally when you
are happy in your new life. That's all I ask.

PAUL:
Come here.

Paul pulls Taylor in for a hug and a kiss.

PAUL:
You've meant more to me than anyone else in the
world these last eight years. I would never do that.
Don't blame yourself. This is my fault. I'm the
asshole. I'm the idiot. You are so fucking awesome,
I don't deserve you. Once you see that, you will be
so happy. I promise. You just need some time away
from me. I promise.

TAYLOR:
I know that isn't true at all but it's nice of you to
say.

PAUL:
Let's not end this vacation on a bad note. I saw we
get rip roaring drunk and go out with a bang!

Paul picks up the bottle of vodka and pours two shots and gives one to Taylor.

TAYLOR:
Ha! Let's toast.

Taylor raises her glass. Paul does the same.

TAYLOR:
To our future plans.

They clink glasses and kiss.

J. Andrew Thomas lives in the suburbs north east of Philadelphia, where he was born. He has a wife, a son and two toy poodles. He has written plays, novels, poetry and short stories which have all been self published.